DIGESTIVE DISORDERS

DIGESTIVE DISORDERS

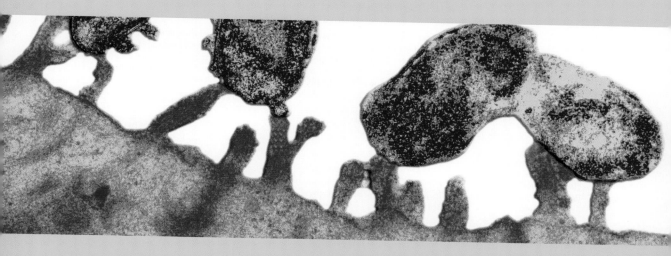

George Capaccio

Marshall Cavendish
Benchmark
New York

With special thanks to Michael J. Smith, MD, MSCE, assistant professor of pediatrics at the University of Louisville School of Medicine, for his expert review of this manuscript.

Library of Congress Cataloging-in-Publication Data

Capaccio, George.
  Digestive disorders / George Capaccio.
    p. cm. — (Health alert)
  Includes index.
  Summary: "Provides comprehensive information on the causes, treatment, and history of digestive disorders"—Provided by publisher.
  ISBN 978-0-7614-4822-8
  1. Digestive organs—Diseases—Juvenile literature. I. Title.
  RC802.C36 2010
  616.99'43—dc22

                                2010003734

Front Cover: A computer illustration showing the digestive system.
Title page: A close-up look at bacteria on stomach cells, which can cause some types of ulcers.

Editor: Joy Bean
Publisher: Michelle Bisson
Art Director: Anahid Hamparian

Photo research by Candlepants Incorporated
Cover Photo: Sebastian Kaulitzki / Alamy Images

The photographs in this book are used by permission and through the courtesy of: *Getty Images*: Veronika Burmeister, 3; 3D Clinic, 5, 34; Nucleus Medical Art, Inc., 11; 3D4Medical.com, 19; David Woolley, 23; Thomas Firak Photography, 26; , 45; Jack Andersen, 49; Elizabeth Simpson, 53; Bek Shakirov, 54; Geoff du Feu, 43. *Alamy Images*: Agencja Free, 7; Hector Aiza / Phototake, 17. *Photo Researchers Inc.*: Astrid & Hanns-Frieder Michler, 14; CNRI, 21; David Mack, 29; John Bavosi, 33; PHANIE, 50. *Art Resource, NY*: Bildarchiv Preussischer Kulturbesitz, 37. *The Bridgeman Art Library*: University Library, Leipzig, Germany/ Archives Charmet, 39.

Printed in Malaysia (T)
6 5 4 3 2 1

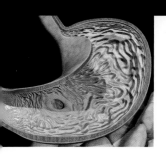

CONTENTS

1

WHAT IS IT LIKE TO HAVE A DIGESTIVE DISORDER?

When Kirsty was fifteen, she had a terrible case of stomach cramps that lasted for three days. Her father took her to the emergency room of a nearby hospital where she underwent a series of tests. When the results of these tests came back, her doctor explained to Kirsty and her family that she had a chronic digestive disorder called **Crohn's disease**. He told them that this disease is a type of **inflammatory bowel disease**, or IBD for short. The word "chronic" at first frightened Kirsty. She thought it meant the disease would cause her to feel extreme pain. She felt a little better when she learned that "chronic" has a very different meaning. It means the disease will never completely leave her body. Symptoms of Crohn's disease will keep coming back throughout her life.

Kirsty began having these symptoms when she was only six. But it took another nine years before she found out what was making her feel sick much of the time. To control her symptoms, she takes about ninety pills each week. She must also go to the hospital on a regular basis to have the doctor

Crohn's disease can be very painful and can cause stomach pains.

examine her blood, her **stool**, and her intestines. One of the symptoms of Crohn's disease that really worries Kirsty is the swelling of her joints, especially in her knees. At first, Kirsty did not know whether it was just growing pains or whether it was something more serious. She said it felt as if something was behind her kneecaps and was forcing them forward.

Kirsty is slowly learning to live with the pain in her joints and her stomach but hopes that one day this pain will go away for good. Until then, she must continue her treatment and periodically undergo **endoscopies**, **colonoscopies**, **MRIs,** and other kinds of tests. Sometimes the stomach cramps are so bad she has to stay in the hospital for a week or longer and take morphine to relieve the pain. While in the hospital, Kirsty is usually not allowed to eat solid food. She gets her meals in liquid form through a tube connected to one of her veins.

As someone with Crohn's disease, Kirsty has many diffi- cult challenges to face. Even though sometimes she feels very depressed, Kirsty is doing her best to live a normal life. "[I] think about suicide often but no matter how bad you feel, there is someone in a worse state than you and they are coping. I am coping."

Crohn's disease is a digestive disorder that affects around one million people in the United States alone. The disease is usually not fatal, but it can be very painful. People who have Crohn's disease may find it hard to lead a normal life. This is especially true for children and teens since the disease may lower their self-esteem and keep them from socializing as much as they would like to. Youngsters with Crohn's disease need the support of their families and friends to help them achieve a satisfying social life.

As Kirsty discovered, the disease is chronic, that is, long-lasting. But it is not constant. There might be times when a person has very mild symptoms or no symptoms at all. When this happens, doctors say the disease is in **remission**. Periods of remission might last weeks, months, even years. But then for no apparent reason the symptoms return. The return of symptoms is called a **flare up**. During a flare up, the disease is very actively present in the body and can cause a great deal of discomfort.

2

WHAT ARE DIGESTIVE DISORDERS?

Our digestive system converts the food we eat into the nutrients our bodies need in order to grow and remain healthy. Digestive disorders are medical problems that affect the gastrointestinal tract, which is part of the digestive system. Most people experience a digestive disorder at least once in their lives. Digestive disorders range from mild and short-lived to painful and long lasting. Understanding how the digestive system works will help us understand what can go wrong and why.

HOW THE DIGESTIVE SYSTEM WORKS

It is lunchtime and you are hungry. All you can think about is food. What will it be today? Roast chicken, mashed potatoes with gravy, a side of your favorite vegetable, apple pie for dessert? Or maybe cheese ravioli, salad, and a slice of home-made bread? Even before you take that first delicious bite, your digestive system is already at work. Sometimes smelling, seeing, or just thinking about certain foods, especially our favorite ones, will make us "lick our chops," or salivate. Tiny glands under the tongue and near the lower jaw produce saliva, a digestive juice. This happens automatically in response to

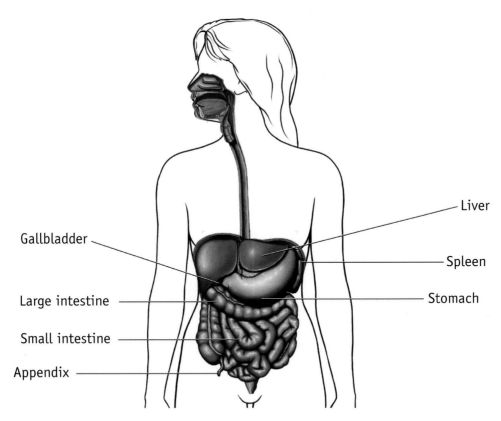

Gallbladder

Liver

Spleen

Large intestine

Stomach

Small intestine

Appendix

Your digestive system is made up of a number of organs, including your stomach, large intestine, and small intestine.

the sight, the taste, or even the thought of food. Our brains send impulses along nerves to the salivary glands telling them to start making saliva. As soon as we start putting food in our mouths, the saliva begins turning it into a watery, mushy mass.

The Gastrointestinal Tract

When we digest our food, we are breaking it down into the nutrients we need in order to stay alive. These nutrients are vitamins, minerals, fats, carbohydrates, proteins, and simple sugars. That chicken you may have had for lunch will not do you much good until it is digested and the proteins in the meat are released into your bloodstream. Food is fuel. It gives us energy and keeps our bodies strong and healthy.

The digestive system begins with the mouth and ends at the anus. In between the two there is a system of organs that handles different phases of the digestive process. When you swallow, a flap of **cartilage** called the **epiglottis** automatically closes over your windpipe so you do not choke on your food. Instead, the food enters the **esophagus**, a tube that connects your throat with your stomach. Muscles along the walls of the esophagus move the food toward the stomach in a series of wavelike motions called **peristalsis**. A valve between the lower end of the esophagus and the stomach opens to let food into the stomach. Then it closes to keep stomach acids and undigested food from going back up the esophagus.

The Stomach

In an average adult the stomach can comfortably hold about 2 to 3 pints (0.9 to 1.4 liters) of food. It produces about an equal amount of digestive acids over a twenty-four-hour period. The stomach does not just hold food. Its powerful muscles continually contract, mixing and mashing solid food. Its acids and digestive juices also destroy germs in contaminated food and begin breaking down food into vital nutrients.

The stomach is a bit like a washing machine. Powerful muscles along the stomach's walls keep churning the food while mixing it with the stomach's own digestive fluids. Once the food becomes more of a liquid than a solid it is ready to move into the small intestine, where most digestion takes place.

The Small Intestine

The small intestine is not really that small. Maybe it should be called the "long intestine," because in a grown-up it is about 22 feet (6.7 meters) long. It is also about 1.5 to 2 inches (3.5 to 5 centimeters) around. The lining of the small intestine is full of specialized projections called **villi** whose job is to absorb nutrients from food. They look like tiny fingers. Projecting from the cells of the small intestine lining are thousands of even smaller projections called microvilli. One square inch of small intestine has about 20,000 villi and ten billion microvilli.

The villi constantly move back and forth as they absorb the

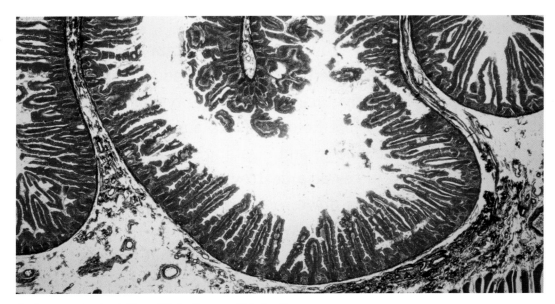

A close-up look at the villi in the small intestine.

nutrients and pass them through the wall of the small intestine and into the bloodstream. Once they enter the bloodstream, these nutrients are able to nourish all parts of our bodies, from our head to our feet and everything in between.

The small intestine cannot do its job without the help of three organs that are not a part of the digestive tract. But without them, digestion would not take place. These organs are the pancreas, the liver, and the gallbladder. The pancreas makes a type of protein known as an **enzyme**. This enzyme travels through pathways, or ducts, from the pancreas into the small intestine, where it helps break down the fats, carbohydrates, and proteins in the food we eat. The liver produces **bile**, a substance that makes it easier for our bodies to absorb fat. The gallbladder stores the bile from the liver until it is needed by the small intestine (in the part called the **duodenum**).

It takes about four hours for the small intestine to digest an average meal, that is, to turn those helpings of chicken, potato, vegetable, and pie into the chemicals we need to keep our bodies alive and healthy.

The Large Intestine

The nutrients that were once your food now pass into the large intestine, which is about 3 to 4 inches (7 to 10 cm) around and 5 feet (1.5 m) long. The large intestine removes water from undigested food and forms solid waste, also known as **feces** or poop, which will eventually be eliminated during a bowel movement.

The large intestine has three main parts. The **cecum** connects the small and large intestines and expands to hold food passing from one to the other. The **appendix** sticks out from the end of the cecum and plays no part in the digestive process. Scientists think it may be an organ left over from earlier stages of human evolution. The **colon** connects with the **rectum**, which collects feces until they are ready to exit the digestive tract through the anus. Sections of the colon also absorb salts and fluids from indigestible food.

DISORDERS OF THE DIGESTIVE SYSTEM

Nearly everyone, from infants to senior citizens, gets an upset stomach at one time or another. This is a common type of digestive disorder that usually goes away by itself or is easily treated. But there are also longer-lasting digestive disorders that can disrupt a person's life and may require strong medication or even hospitalization and, in some cases, surgery. Digestive disorders are usually ailments of the gastrointestinal tract, which runs from the mouth to the anus and includes the esophagus, stomach, small and large intestines, and related organs such as the pancreas and gallbladder. These disorders range from mild to very severe. Mild digestive disorders include indigestion, heartburn, **diarrhea**, and **constipation.** More serious disorders of the digestive tract include **acid reflux**, **celiac disease**, **irritable bowel syndrome** (IBS), **ulcers**, inflammatory bowel disease (IBD), and certain types of cancer.

Fortunately, there is help for people suffering from digestive disorders. Taking the proper medication, eating a healthy diet, reducing stress, and exercising more can ease or even eliminate many of the symptoms.

Acid Reflux: A Disease of the Esophagus

Have you ever felt a burning sensation in your chest after you have eaten something? This feeling is sometimes called heart-burn. Actually, it has nothing at all to do with the heart. It is the result of acid in your stomach splashing back up into your esophagus, which lacks the stomach's protective lining. This splash back happens when the muscle controlling the opening between the esophagus and the stomach fails to keep this opening closed or does not close it tightly enough. Acid in the esophagus causes inflammation, which we experience as a burning sensation, or heartburn. Occasional acid reflux by itself is not a disorder. But if it happens frequently or lasts a long time, it can lead to

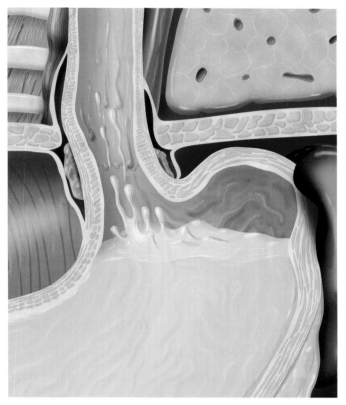

This computer illustration shows acid reflux, in which acidic stomach contents move up into the esophagus.

problems in the esophagus. One such problem is ulcers, which are sores that do not heal. Acid reflux can also cause the tissue that is lining the walls of the esophagus to become scarred. Scar tissue narrows the inside of the esophagus. When this happens, it becomes difficult to swallow food and liquids. If the problem becomes too severe, a person may need surgery.

The medical term for inflammation of the esophagus is gastroesophageal reflux disease (**GERD**). For most people, taking an over-the-counter antacid such as Tums or Maalox will relieve the heartburn associated with this disorder. People who are sensitive to certain foods may have to eliminate them from their diet or at least eat fewer of them. Foods that are known to cause acid reflux include chocolate, tomatoes, caffeinated drinks such as coffee, and citrus fruits and juices.

Constipation and Diarrhea

Constipation and diarrhea are two of the most common digestive disorders. They usually do not last very long and have no harmful effects on the digestive system. When you have diarrhea, your poop is loose and watery, and you have to go to the bathroom several times during the day. Diarrhea happens when the muscles inside the intestines contract too quickly. They do not leave enough time for water to be absorbed into the bloodstream. Partially digested food and liquids in the large intestine rush toward the nearest exit, which happens to be the anus.

If you do not wash your hands after going to the bathroom and then touch the food you eat, germs on your hands can give you diarrhea. You can also get diarrhea from medicines or foods that your body cannot tolerate. Another cause is an infection in the intestines or in some other part of the body. Food or water that contains harmful types of bacteria, viruses,

E. Coli Infection

Some digestive disorders are the result of bacteria. Bacteria are microscopic germs that are invisible to the human eye. E. coli is a type of bacteria known to cause diarrhea, terrible cramps, and sometimes vomiting in people who ingest contaminated food or water. E. coli stands for Escherichia coli. Diarrhea caused by E. coli is sometimes referred to as "traveler's diarrhea" since it often happens to people who visit countries where there is poor sanitation.

Uncooked or undercooked beef may contain E. coli bacteria from infected cattle. E. coli can also pass from person to person. This may happen if you eat food that has been handled by an infected person. If that person has not washed his or her hands with soap after using the toilet, then you might get the germ, too, and become sick.

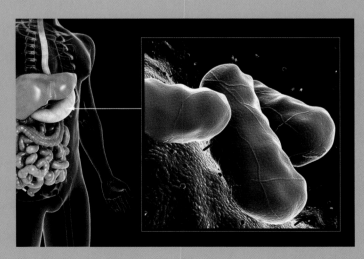

A computer illustration of E. coli bacteria as seen through a microscope.

or parasites can produce severe diarrhea, often with cramps, nausea, and vomiting. Diarrhea that lasts more than a few days can cause dehydration, which happens when the body does not have enough fluid. Children and older people who become dehydrated from chronic or long-lasting diarrhea may become dangerously sick.

Constipation is the opposite of diarrhea. Constipation happens when feces move too slowly through the digestive tract. This allows plenty of time for more and more water to be absorbed into the bloodstream, causing feces to become drier and more compact. They pile up in the rectum and become harder to pass, sometimes for several days or longer. A person who is constipated has to strain in order to have a bowel movement.

Not getting enough exercise and not drinking enough fluids are two leading causes of constipation. Other causes include eating foods that are lacking in fiber and skipping opportunities to have a bowel movement when the urge is felt.

Irritable Bowel Syndrome (IBS)

Our small and large intestines make up what doctors call the **bowel**. During digestion, muscles in the walls of the bowel automatically contract. This movement, controlled by the brain, keeps food and fluids moving along. If the muscles move too quickly, food is not properly digested and diarrhea may result.

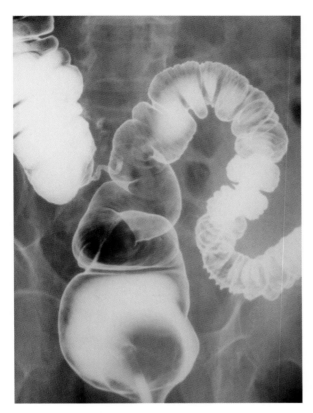

This colored X-ray shows irritable bowel syndrome. The rectum (lower center) is distended due to constipation or a buildup of gases.

If the muscles move too slowly, too much water is absorbed. The stool becomes hard and difficult to pass. In other words, a person feels constipated.

Someone with irritable bowel syndrome may have abnormal muscle contractions in their intestines. This can produce repeated bouts of either diarrhea or constipation or both. Other symptoms of IBS are mucus in the stool, cramps, excessive gas, and **bloating** in the abdomen, which includes the stomach and the intestines.

People of all ages can have IBS. One recent study shows that about 6 percent of middle school students and 14 percent of high school students have experienced the symptoms of IBS.

Although the exact cause is not known, medical researchers have come up with a few possible explanations: food allergies, too much bacteria in the colon, emotional stress, and a glitch

Helpful Worms

. . . .

Could worms help someone with an inflammatory bowel disease? A team of medical researchers thinks the answer might be yes. Recently, the researchers got together a group of people with Crohn's disease to see if their idea would work. They gave the people in the group a drink containing microscopic worm eggs. The eggs traveled to the small intestine where they hatched. Several months later, when the study was over, the results were very encouraging. Three-quarters of the people felt better. Their symptoms practically vanished.

The worms used in the experiment were not the kind used to bait fishing hooks. They belonged to a group of parasites called helminths, which include hookworms and roundworms. These worms are able to live in people's intestines. In many poor parts of the world, where sanitation is inadequate, children often become infected with worm parasites. In developed countries, improvements in sanitation and the use of de-worming medications have meant that fewer and fewer kids are getting worms.

People with Crohn's disease may have immune systems that are not working properly. Instead of attacking harmful bacteria or viruses, the immune system attacks healthy tissue inside the digestive tract. The tissue becomes inflamed, and the person develops symptoms. But if worm parasites are present, the immune system has something to defend the body against. Instead of destroying healthy tissue, it will go after the worms. While the results of this experiment are promising, there is still no cure for Crohn's disease or other kinds of inflammatory bowel disease.

in the way the brain and the digestive tract exchange information. So far there is no cure for IBS. Fortunately, it is not fatal and will not harm the intestines, and the symptoms are treatable.

Celiac Disease

A person with celiac disease cannot tolerate **gluten**. Gluten is a protein found in certain medicines, vitamin supplements, and even lip balms and the glue used on postage stamps. Grains such as wheat, barley, and rye also contain gluten. Flours made from these grains are used to make many of the foods we

Gluten is the protein that helps make pizza dough stretchy. People with celiac disease have an allergy to gluten.

enjoy, such as pasta, breakfast cereals, pretzels, muffins, and bread. Bread or pizza dough can be stretched because of the gluten in the flour.

When someone with celiac disease eats a food containing gluten, his or her immune system is triggered in a harmful way. It starts to destroy the villi inside the small intestine. These microscopic structures absorb nutrients from digested food and pass them into the bloodstream to nourish all parts of the body. If the villi are destroyed, which is what happens with celiac disease, the person risks becoming malnourished because he or she is not getting enough of the nutrients the body requires, no matter how much food is eaten. Scientists now know that celiac disease is hereditary. It is passed down through families from one generation to the next. Sometimes a person who has the disease may not show any symptoms until he or she becomes an adult. Then an infection, emotional stress, childbirth, or surgery can cause the disease to become active. Infants and young children with celiac disease are likely to experience symptoms in their digestive systems. These include constipation, chronic diarrhea, abdominal pain, intestinal bloating, vomiting, and bad-smelling stool. Adults are more likely to have symptoms in other parts of their bodies. Tiredness, bone or joint pain, depression, bone loss, numbness in the feet and hands, and canker sores in the mouth are among the signs of celiac disease in adults.

Additional symptoms of celiac disease include muscle cramps and weight loss. The surest way to control the symptoms of celiac disease is to switch to a gluten-free diet.

Lactose Intolerance

Lactose is a sugar found in milk and other dairy products made from milk such as cheese and ice cream. An enzyme made in the small intestine breaks down lactose into simple sugars that are easily absorbed into the bloodstream. People who are **lactose intolerant** have an insufficient amount of this enzyme, which is called **lactase.** Their digestive systems are unable to absorb lactose, which remains in the abdomen. When they eat or drink foods containing lactose, they experience uncomfortable symptoms. Symptoms do not start immediately. It may take up to two hours before a person feels sick. Symptoms vary from mild to severe and include cramps, nausea, gas, diarrhea, and bloating.

For most children, lactose intolerance is not a problem since children are usually born with enough lactase. But some people, as they get older, become lactose intolerant when their bodies can no longer produce enough of the lactase enzyme.

Researchers have found that lactose intolerance, like celiac disease, is often genetic. Some people who cannot digest lactose probably inherited this condition from their parents. Injury to the small intestine and digestive disorders such as

The lactose in dairy products makes some people feel ill. This is because their bodies do not make enough of the enzyme lactase, which helps people digest dairy products.

celiac disease, inflammatory bowel disease, and Crohn's disease can also cause a shortage of lactase.

Doctors used to advise people with lactose intolerance to avoid all dairy products. But this is no longer the case. Dairy products contain calcium, a mineral that helps keep our bones strong and healthy throughout our lives. Children and teenagers, whose bones are still growing, need an adequate supply of calcium in their diet. Because dairy products are a rich source of calcium, the American Academy of Pediatrics has established new guidelines for treating lactose intolerance. Doctors now recommend that people with this disorder try different dairy foods to see which ones cause fewer symptoms.

Inflammatory Bowel Disease (IBD)

This condition is somewhat similar to irritable bowel syndrome. But inflammatory bowel disease is much more serious. The symptoms of IBD can be very painful and long lasting. Crohn's disease and **ulcerative colitis** are the two major types of inflammatory bowel disease. Both diseases cause inflammation in the small and large

Lactose Intolerance and Heredity

Lactose intolerance affects certain ethnic and racial groups more than others. People whose ancestors came from northern Europe are much less likely to have this disorder. On the other hand, a higher percentage of African Americans, Native American Indians, and Asian Americans are lactose intolerant.

One possible reason for this difference is that many non-European cultures do not have a history of consuming dairy products. The genetic makeup of people from these cultures has developed along different lines. Their intestines are genetically programmed to stop producing the lactase enzyme usually in early childhood. So they become lactose intolerant when they get older.

Drinking Cow's Milk

. . . .

Some people have a bad reaction to drinking milk from cows. The symptoms are similar to those of lactose intolerance. But cow's milk intolerance is an allergic reaction. It is not the same as lactose intolerance, which is a digestive disorder.

intestines. Ulcerative colitis only affects the inner lining of the colon and the rectum. Crohn's disease goes deeper into the intestinal wall and usually shows up in the **ileum**, which is the part of the small intestine that connects with the large intestine. But the disease can also occur in other parts of the digestive system, from the mouth to the **anus**. Because these two types of IBD have many symptoms in common, doctors must be very careful when making a diagnosis.

Symptoms of Crohn's disease range from mild to severe and include abdominal pain, fever, loss of appetite, weight loss, and chronic diarrhea, sometimes with blood, mucus, or pus in the stool. The disease can also involve symptoms that have nothing to do with the digestive tract. For instance, Kirsty in Chapter One experienced pain in her joints, especially her knees. The pain and swelling in her knees were symptoms of Crohn's disease. Skin lesions and sores inside the mouth are other kinds of symptoms not related to the digestive tract.

People who have this particular digestive disorder are not alike in the way they experience their illness or in how they

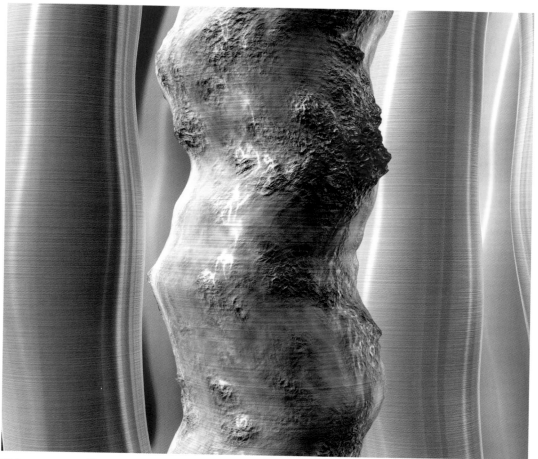

This computer illustration shows the lining of the intestines. Inflammatory bowel diseases causes inflammation, ulceration, and thickening (all shown in red) of the intestinal lining.

respond to medication. Some individuals might suffer very painful stomach cramps during a flare up while for others a flare up might only be slightly uncomfortable. Similarly, one drug might be very effective in reducing symptoms for some but ineffective for others.

Medical researchers have not yet discovered the cause of Crohn's disease. It may have something to do with **heredity** since the disease appears to run in families. About 20 to 25 percent of people with the disease have a relative who has some form of IBD. The disease also tends to show up more in some ethnic groups than in others. It mainly affects people living in highly developed societies such as those found in the West. Scientists think this may have something to do with the kinds of food people in these societies eat or the conditions of their environment. But much more research needs to be done to understand how diet and environment may contribute to Crohn's disease.

Crohn's disease is considered a disease of the **immune system**. When the body is trying to heal itself from a wound or an infection, it causes tissues to swell and become inflamed. Inflammation is therefore a natural response. But in Crohn's disease and ulcerative colitis, parts of the digestive tract become chronically inflamed. So far, scientists do not know what triggers this immune response.

The good news is that scientists are learning more and

more about the relationship between the disease and a person's genetic makeup and what role the environment plays in triggering a flare up. New drugs, advances in surgery, and experimental kinds of treatment promise to relieve many of the symptoms of inflammatory bowel disease.

Ulcerative colitis is the other form of inflammatory bowel disease. It affects the inner lining of the colon and the rectum, which make up the lower portions of the large intestine. Symptoms of ulcerative colitis include diarrhea, loss of appetite, tiredness, weight loss, and bleeding from the rectum. Besides causing inflammation, ulcerative colitis also causes open sores to form in the affected areas. These sores, or ulcers, are responsible for the bleeding that occurs during bowel movements. If the bleeding is excessive, it can lead to **anemia,** a disorder in which the body has a decreased amount of red blood cells.

People between the ages of fifteen and thirty are more likely to develop ulcerative colitis than either children or older people. Males are just as likely to develop this disorder as females. In some families, the disease seems to be inherited. As with Crohn's disease, there is no known cause and no cure. Symptoms can be managed with proper treatment. In some cases, doctors may recommend surgery to remove the colon if symptoms have become too severe. Ulcerative colitis is rarely fatal. However, it can lead to a greater risk of colon cancer if it spreads throughout the large intestine.

Crohn's Disease and Ulcerative Colitis: Differences and Similarities

Crohn's Disease	Shared Characteristics	Ulcerative Colitis
Can affect any part of the digestive tract, including the mouth, esophagus, stomach, and small intestine.	Both are types of inflammatory bowel disease.	Only affects the large intestine.
Affects the deeper layers of the intestinal wall.	Both cause redness and swelling in the affected areas.	Only affects the inner lining of the large intestine.
	Both may be related to the body's immune system.	
	Both have similar symptoms, including diarrhea, abdominal pain, and fever.	
	Both are chronic, lifelong diseases.	
	Both are rarely fatal.	

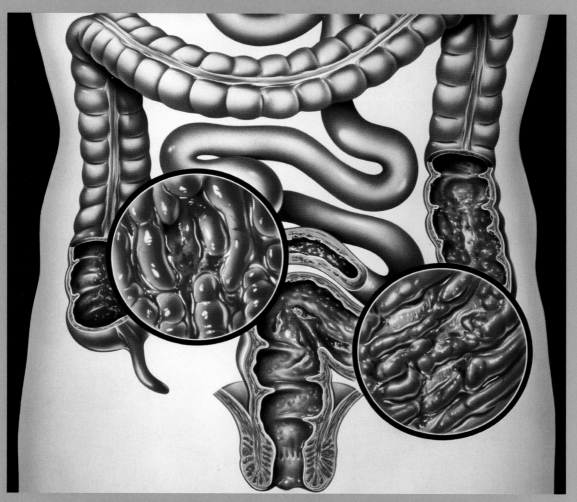

This computer illustration shows the small intestine affected by Crohn's disease (circle on the left) and ulcerative colitis (circle on the right).

ULCERS

Ulcers are sores that develop in the lining of the digestive tract. The three most common locations of ulcers are the esophagus, the stomach, and the upper portion of the small intestine (the duodenum). People with ulcers usually experience a burning sensation and may not experience any other symptoms. But if the ulcers become too deep, they can cause

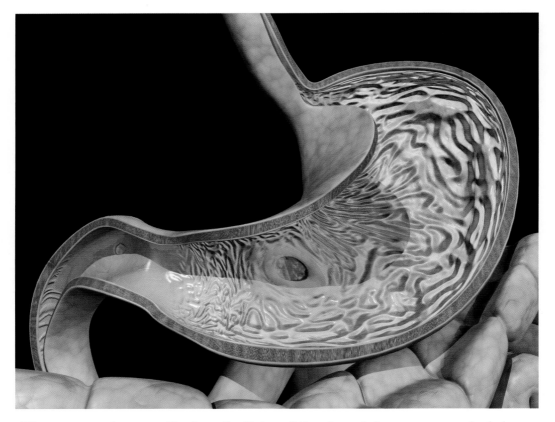

When someone has a peptic ulcer, the lining of the stomach is worn away and a hole forms.

more serious problems such as internal bleeding. Stomach ulcers can also make it difficult for food to pass into the small intestine. If this happens, then the person with stomach ulcers may become malnourished and start to lose too much weight.

At one time, doctors thought ulcers were caused by stress or by eating foods that are very spicy. But medical research has shown this to be untrue. Emotional stress and spicy foods will not cause ulcers, but they can make the symptoms worse. Doctors now know that a leading cause of ulcers is an infection. A germ called **Helicobacter pylori** (or H. pylori for short) is responsible for the infection. Surprisingly, about half of the world's population is infected with H. pylori, but only some of the people infected with H. pylori actually develop ulcers. With improvements in hygiene and sanitation, at least in some parts of the world, young people are far less likely to become infected. Another cause of ulcers is having too much stomach acid, which can damage the lining of the digestive tract. Certain anti-inflammatory medicines, if taken frequently over a long period of time, can cause ulcers to form in the stomach lining. These medicines include over-the-counter drugs such as aspirin and ibuprofen, and some types of drugs that doctors prescribe for arthritis.

3

HISTORY OF DIGESTIVE DISORDERS

Medical science continues to find more effective ways of diagnosing and treating digestive disorders. Most of these disorders are not new. They have a long history that probably goes back thousands of years to the beginnings of human civilization. So how did our distant ancestors deal with the occasional bout of diarrhea or constipation, or a painful bellyache? Thanks to historical accounts that have survived the centuries, we know something about how people long ago treated digestive disorders. Of course, as we get closer to the present, there is much more information available to help us understand how treatments have changed over time.

Just about every culture has developed its own methods of treating digestive disorders. The ancient civilizations of Egypt,

China, and India, for instance, have long histories of devising cures for these disorders. The same is true for Native American Indian cultures of North and South America. In the nineteenth century, many American families who lived in rural areas might have had to travel great distances in order to see a doctor. If someone in the family got sick or was injured, it made more sense to treat the problem with the help of a manual on diseases. A popular manual in the late 1800s was *The Practical Home Physician*. This medical book prescribed remedies for

This page from a medical book from the fourteenth century shows chamomile is used for stomach pains.

many different diseases, including digestive disorders. Each disease was carefully described so families could make their own diagnosis without the aid of a doctor.

Many of the remedies for digestive disorders could be prepared in the home with the use of ordinary ingredients such as herbs, plant oils, or special spices. Others called for dietary changes in addition to the use of various homemade medicines.

Some of these old-fashioned remedies may still be beneficial. But for the most part, because of advances in medical science, they are out-of-date and no longer prescribed.

HEARTBURN

When you have heartburn, you do not have to worry that your heart is on fire. What is happening is that stomach acid is finding its way into your esophagus and causing a burning sensation. Back in the 1800s, if you had heartburn, your family might have followed the advice of *The Practical Home Physician*. First, they might have given you a pinch of baking powder. If that did not relieve your heartburn, you could have tried a half tablespoon of limewater, which works as an antacid. If these remedies failed, then a stronger cure was five to ten drops of chloroform mixed with a teaspoon of brandy or whiskey. (Chloroform is a very dangerous chemical in liquid form. In the past, it was used to put patients to sleep before surgery. Prolonged exposure can lead to cancer and other diseases.)

CONSTIPATION AND DIARRHEA

In ancient Egypt, when a very rich and powerful person died, the body was preserved in a special way. It became a mummy. The process of turning corpses into mummies taught Egyptians a great deal about the human body. Much of this knowledge has been preserved in scrolls made of papyrus, a plant that grows along the Nile River in Egypt. In the nineteenth century, archaeologists discovered what turned out to be one of the oldest medical textbooks in the world. It was written in Egyptian hieroglyphics more than three thousand years ago and may be a copy of a much older document. Known as the *Ebers Papyrus*, it contains remedies for everything from a scorpion's sting to a crushed skull.

A sample page from the *Ebers Papyrus* from 1550 B.C.E. Ancient Egyptians turned to this book for help in healing themselves of many ailments.

Imagine that you were living in ancient Egypt during the building of the great pyramids. One day you wake up with a bad case of diarrhea. It is so bad you cannot go to school to learn your hieroglyphics. Your mother might prepare a special food to stop the diarrhea. The recipe for this food comes from the book *Ebers Papyrus*. It consists of figs and grapes, some bread dough, corn, and onion, a fruit called elderberry, and a sprinkling of good, wholesome dirt.

Like people in many other cultures, ancient Egyptians believed certain herbs and plants had healing powers. To treat digestive disorders, they made herbal remedies from the leaves, roots, or stems of these plants. For diarrhea, the *Ebers Papyrus* prescribes plants such as acacia, bayberry (also prescribed to soothe ulcers and shrink hemorrhoids), henna, myrrh, and sandalwood. For constipation, the book has remedies containing garlic, licorice root, and fruit from the tamarind tree. If an Egyptian doctor thought the constipation was a symptom of ulcers, then he might have prescribed syrup made from sweet ale (an alcoholic drink) and flour.

EARTH EATERS

Doctors in ancient Egypt sometimes prescribed remedies that included ordinary soil. There is actually a long history of making medicine from materials taken directly from the earth. Naturally occurring clay is a good example. In some cultures, people have eaten clay in order to treat indigestion, diarrhea, and stomach pain. For example, clay that is rich in sodium bicarbonate is supposedly good for indigestion. Ordinary baking soda is a common form of sodium bicarbonate, which is sometimes taken as an antacid.

Clays containing chemicals such as magnesium oxide and magnesium hydroxide have also been eaten for stomach upsets. Today these same chemicals go into making popular medications such as Mylanta, Maalox, and Phillips' Milk of Magnesia.

People who are lactose intolerant need to take calcium supplements in order to keep their bones and teeth healthy.

An important source of this mineral is calcium carbonate, which can be taken in tablet or liquid form. Calcium carbonate is also a major ingredient in antacids such as Tums and Rolaids. The mineral is found in nature as chalk. In the past, before modern medicine, people could eat naturally occurring chalk to give their bellies the benefits of calcium carbonate. (At one time, classroom chalk was made from chalk found in nature, but that is no longer the case.)

STOMACH PAIN AND INDIGESTION

The ancient Egyptians had a very unique remedy for indigestion. They advised patients to crush the tooth of a hog, put the crushed tooth inside of four sugar cakes, and eat one cake a day for four days.

More than three hundred years ago an English doctor named Nicholas Culpeper published a book on remedies using plants and herbs. His book is called *Culpeper's Complete Herbal.* For stomach pain and indigestion, he prescribed soups or teas made from plants such as caraway, horse parsley, and barley.

Cayenne pepper has also played an important role in treating digestive disorders. Its use goes back thousands of years. In powder form, cayenne pepper makes food taste hot and spicy. But as a digestive aid, small amounts have been used to improve digestion and stimulate muscle movement in the intestines.

Peppermint and chamomile are two more old-fashioned

Colicky Babies

. . . .

Babies who cry for long periods of time are said to have colic. Doctors consider this to be normal for some babies. Even though the exact cause of colic remains unknown, doctors do not think it is the result of digestive problems, illness, or pain. Fortunately for parents with colicky babies, the condition is temporary. It usually goes away when the child is between eight and fourteen weeks of age.

remedies for stomach pain and indigestion. Chemicals in both herbs may help reduce pain and soothe stomach upset. Teas made from these plants are still popular today.

COLIC

Colic in adults is the name given to a sudden, sharp pain in the abdomen, which includes the stomach and the intestines. In the 1800s, families could open a copy of *The Practical Home Physician* and find several different methods for treating colic. The remedy for mild pain was placing hot cloths on the person's abdomen and giving him or her a tablespoon of brandy or whiskey with some ginger spice. For severe pain, then the book recommended a dose of opium, a highly addictive drug that is now illegal. Opium was also used as a laxative to cause a bowel movement. In those days, it was commonly believed that a complete bowel movement would keep the colic from coming back. If the opium failed to work, then the person with colic was advised to have an **enema**. Squeezing warm water with castor oil or soapsuds into the rectum would do the trick, according to *The Practical Home Physician*.

IRRITABLE BOWEL SYNDROME

The Practical Home Physician included a treatment for what was then known as "inflammation of the bowels." Today we call this disorder inflammatory bowel disease (IBD). The nineteenth-century cure involved sprinkling turpentine on hot, damp cloths and placing these on the abdomen. Instead of hot cloths, a mustard paste could also be used to stop the inflammation. If there was abdominal pain, then regular doses of opium were prescribed.

Poppies

· · · · · · · · · · · ·

Opium is derived from a certain type of poppy flower. The natural chemicals that make up opium go into making substances such as morphine and heroin. Morphine is an anesthetic, or pain killer, used in hospitals for people with severe pain.

This poppy flower contains some of the ingredients that go into making opium.

4

DIAGNOSING, TREATING, AND PREVENTING DIGESTIVE DISORDERS

People with digestive disorders no longer have to rely on home remedies such as those found in *The Practical Home Physician*. Modern medical science has developed new ways to diagnose, treat, and in some cases prevent these disorders.

ACID REFLUX

A sure sign of acid reflux is when sour-tasting food or liquid in the stomach frequently comes back into the mouth. Doctors have various methods for determining how serious the problem is. They can have the patient swallow a chalky-colored solution that contains **barium**. This chemical coats the walls of the stomach and esophagus. When X-rays of the digestive tract are taken, the barium reveals any signs of acid reflux and other abnormalities such as ulcers or **hernias**.

Another method is to lower a tube through the nose and into the esophagus. The tube, or catheter, is coated with an acid-sensitive substance that can detect and measure acid reflux.

A third method is to perform an endoscopy. For this procedure, the doctor inserts a device called a scope through the patient's mouth. The scope has a

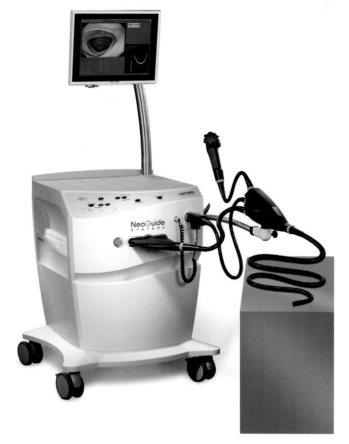

A new endoscopy system helps doctors diagnose a number of conditions in patients, including acid reflux.

small light at one end. The light allows the doctor to see if there is any inflammation in the esophagus.

People with acid reflux can take antacids to reduce the symptoms. They can also raise the head of their bed to keep partly digested food from coming up while they sleep. If the problem is long lasting, then a doctor might prescribe medication to decrease the amount of acid in the stomach. If acid reflux has caused scar tissue to form inside the esophagus and the patient has difficulty swallowing, then surgery might be necessary.

There are some things you can do to prevent acid reflux:

- Eat moderate amounts of food at mealtimes.
- Avoid eating within two or three hours of going to bed.
- Leave time for your food to digest before you exercise.
- If you are overweight, try to lose weight.
- If you smoke, then stop.
- If you do not smoke, then do not start.
- Limit how much coffee you drink.
- If possible, avoid caffeinated beverages.

IRRITABLE BOWEL SYNDROME

In order to diagnose irritable bowel syndrome, a doctor will first learn everything possible about the person's medical history. Next, the doctor will give the patient a complete physical exam. After ruling out other diseases, such as inflammatory bowel disease (IBD), the doctor may give the patient a barium enema. The barium will allow X-rays to capture a clear image of the large intestine. If necessary, the doctor may use a scope to view part or all of the large intestine.

Eating a low-fat diet can reduce symptoms. High-fiber foods such as raw fruits and vegetables may also reduce symptoms. However, for some people a diet that includes lots of high-fiber foods can actually make symptoms worse, so people with

IBS should experiment to see how their bodies react to fiber.

Because emotional stress can trigger symptoms, doctors advise people with IBS to find ways to reduce stress and relax. Psychological counseling is one way. Meditation, yoga, and moderate exercise are other ways to reduce stress.

For constipation and diarrhea—two of the leading symptoms of IBS—doctors may prescribe either laxatives or antidiarrheal medications. So far, medical researchers have not found a way to prevent irritable bowel syndrome from developing.

LACTOSE INTOLERANCE

A person whose stomach becomes upset soon after drinking milk or consuming a dairy product may be lactose intolerant. However, many of the symptoms of this disorder are similar to symptoms of other digestive disorders, such as irritable bowel syndrome. To make a positive diagnosis, a doctor can administer various tests. The most common tests are the lactose intolerance test, the hydrogen breath test, and the stool acidity test. All three tests measure how well the patient's digestive system is able to absorb lactose.

For the lactose intolerance test, a person swallows a liquid containing lactose. A nurse or physician's assistant then takes samples of his or her blood over a two-hour period. The samples, when analyzed, measure the amount of glucose in the blood. If the lactase enzyme is breaking down the lactose, then glucose levels should increase and the person is not lactose intolerant. But if glucose levels stay the same, then the lactose is not breaking down. This suggests that the person is lactose intolerant.

Another reliable test for this disorder is the hydrogen breath test. As in the first test, the person drinks a liquid containing lactose. If the lactose is not properly digested, it will remain in the large intestine. Bacteria in the large intestine go to work on the undigested lactose, causing it to ferment. In the process, a variety of gases are released. One of these gases is hydrogen. The hydrogen enters the bloodstream and is carried to the lungs where it is exhaled. Normally, a person's breath does not contain very much hydrogen. In the hydrogen breath test, a raised level of hydrogen in the breath is evidence that the person is lactose intolerant.

Infants and young children are not given either the lactose intolerance test or the hydrogen breath test. Instead, their stool is tested to measure the amount of acid present. Undigested lactose in the large intestine undergoes fermentation by bacteria. Besides producing gases such as hydrogen, this process also creates **lactic acid**. By measuring the amount of lactic acid in the stool, a doctor can determine if the child is lactose intolerant.

Medical science has still not found a way to prevent lactose intolerance or to improve the body's ability to make the lactase enzyme. However, proper treatment can keep symptoms from occurring. The key is diet. Some people with this disorder can tolerate only small amounts of lactose in their diet. One glass of milk may cause them to develop symptoms. They will have to watch what they eat very carefully and avoid or eliminate many dairy products. Other people may be able to tolerate much greater amounts of lactose, so their diet may be less restrictive.

Since no one reacts to lactose the same way, people may need to experiment to find out which lactose-containing foods their bodies can handle and which ones produce symptoms. People who are very sensitive to lactose may

People who have problem digesting lactose can get sick by drinking a single glass of milk.

take lactase in tablet or liquid form before eating. This enzyme will help their bodies digest the lactose in the foods or beverages they consume.

Another way to prevent symptoms is to eat smaller amounts of foods with lactose at any one time. Infants and young children who are lactose intolerant should not be given formulas or foods containing lactose until their digestive systems have developed. Older children and adults can include lactose in their diet but need to be careful about the types and amounts of foods they consume.

CELIAC DISEASE

Some symptoms of celiac disease are similar to those of other diseases such as inflammatory bowel disease, intestinal infections, and anemia. For this reason, doctors may not realize the patient has celiac disease. But thanks to more accurate blood tests, more people are being correctly diagnosed with this digestive disorder.

People who have celiac disease can still eat pasta, but they need to look for pasta that is gluten-free. This symbol shows that this pasta was made without wheat, which is the ingredient that contains gluten in pasta.

Normally, proteins called **antibodies** protect the body from harmful viruses or bacteria. Other kinds of antibodies called **autoantibodies** attack healthy cells and tissues in the body. A person with celiac disease has high levels of certain autoantibodies in his or her blood.

If these high levels show up in a blood test, then the doctor will make a diagnosis of celiac disease.

To make sure the correct diagnosis has been made, the doctor can perform a **biopsy** of the small intestine. This is done by gently inserting a long, thin tube called an endoscope through the patient's mouth and esophagus and into the small intestine. A special instrument passed through the tube allows the doctor to remove a small part of the lining. This tissue sample will later be analyzed for signs of damage to the villi.

A person with celiac disease must cut out all sources of gluten from his or her diet. This means no foods containing wheat, rye, or barley, and no food products made from these grains. Pasta, cereal, bread, sweets, and many processed foods, if they contain gluten, must be avoided. Hidden sources of gluten such as soy sauce and food preservatives must also be avoided.

A dietician can help a person with celiac disease make the changes that will lead to health. Many people may find it difficult to make these changes. Favorite snacks or breakfast cereals made with wheat, for instance, might be hard to give up. But with the support of family, friends, and health care professionals, people can learn how to live with a gluten-free diet. They will need to pay greater attention to ingredients listed on food labels and learn which foods are safe to eat. When they go out to eat or order lunch at school or work, they will have to be sure the foods they select are gluten-free.

However, people with celiac disease do not need to feel deprived. They can still eat fruit, vegetables, fish, poultry, and meat, as long as these foods are not prepared with anything containing gluten. There are also many different kinds of gluten-free breads, pasta, and cereal available in grocery stores and supermarkets. Other carbohydrates that are not a problem include corn, potatoes, rice, and grains such as quinoa, buckwheat, and small amounts of oats.

Science has not discovered a cure for celiac disease, but following a gluten-free diet will prevent symptoms in most people and will heal any damage to the small intestine as a result of this disease.

FOOD FOR THOUGHT

Probably the most effective way to prevent or manage common digestive disorders is to eat a healthy diet. However that is not always as easy as it may sound. There is plenty of disagreement about what is and is not a healthy diet. Some guidelines for healthy eating have been overly influenced by the food industry, which may wish to promote certain types of foods. Other guidelines overlook the latest research into the connection between diet and health.

The U.S. Department of Food and Agriculture (USDA) came up with the concept of a food guide pyramid in the 1990s. Foods at the base of the pyramid were supposed to make up the bulk of a person's diet. These included bread, cereal, rice, and pasta. Foods at the very top included fats, oils, and sweets, which were to be eaten in moderation.

The federal government publishes a new set of guidelines for healthy eating every five years. These guidelines are supposed to help average Americans decide which foods to eat and which ones to avoid. The guidelines also help public schools plan their lunch menus. The USDA's food pyramid is based on these guidelines.

In 2005, the USDA revised its thinking about what makes up a healthy diet and created a new illustration called MyPyramid. On one side there are six colored stripes. Each color stands for a different food group.

The old food pyramid shows that grains and bread should make up the majority of a person's diet and fats and oils should be used sparingly.

For instance, orange represents grains. Purple stands for meat and beans. The wider the color band the more of that particular food group should be eaten to maintain a balanced diet, according to the USDA.

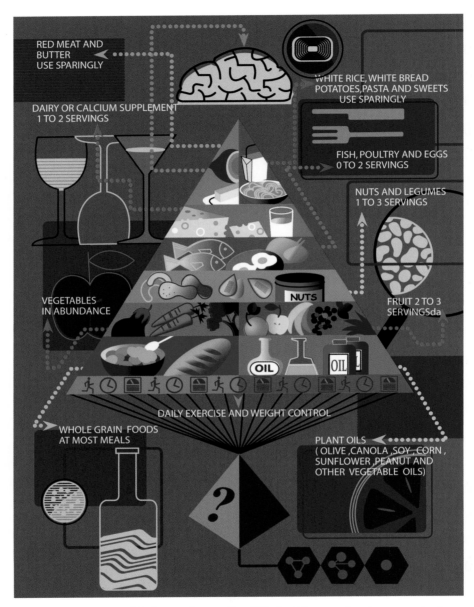

RED MEAT AND
BUTTER
USE SPARINGLY

WHITE RICE, WHITE BREAD
POTATOES, PASTA AND SWEETS
USE SPARINGLY

DAIRY OR CALCIUM SUPPLEMENT
1 TO 2 SERVINGS

FISH, POULTRY AND EGGS
0 TO 2 SERVINGS

NUTS AND LEGUMES
1 TO 3 SERVINGS

VEGETABLES
IN ABUNDANCE

NUTS

FRUIT 2 TO 3
SERVINGSda

DAILY EXERCISE AND WEIGHT CONTROL

WHOLE GRAIN FOODS
AT MOST MEALS

PLANT OILS
(OLIVE ,CANOLA ,SOY , CORN ,
SUNFLOWER ,PEANUT AND
OTHER VEGETABLE OILS)

?

The new food pyramid shows that a diet filled with a moderate amount of grains, oils, proteins, fats, and fruits and vegetables is the best way to have a balanced diet.

Recently, the Harvard School of Public Health published its own version of the food pyramid. Called the Healthy Eating Pyramid, it reflects the most up-to-date findings on nutrition. This new food pyramid rests on a base of daily exercise and weight control. Nutritionists have found that exercise influences what a person eats and how food, in turn, affects health. Someone following the Healthy Eating Pyramid guidelines should eat only small amounts of red meat, butter, white rice, potatoes, pasta, sweets, and sugary drinks. These foods are known to increase blood sugar, which can result in weight gain, diabetes, heart disease, and other long-term disorders. Otherwise, these new guidelines recommend eating plenty of whole grains, healthy fats and oils, and fresh vegetables and fruits.

The food we eat has a lot to do with how well or how poorly our digestive system functions. By choosing healthy foods, we can manage or prevent some of the more common digestive disorders such as heartburn, constipation, and diarrhea. A nutritious, well-balanced diet can also help control the symptoms of more serious disorders such as ulcers, irritable bowel syndrome, and inflammatory bowel disease.

Besides eating nutritious foods, we need to get plenty of exercise and find ways to reduce the stress in our lives. Taken together, these lifestyle improvements will help us maintain a healthy digestive system for life.

GLOSSARY

acid reflux—A digestive disorder in which stomach acid splashes back up into the esophagus and causes a burning sensation commonly called heartburn.

anemia—A medical condition that results when blood lacks enough red blood cells or these cells do not have enough hemoglobin, an iron-carrying protein.

antibodies—Proteins produced in the body in response to harmful bacteria or virus.

anus—The opening at the end of the large intestine through which feces are passed.

appendix—The narrow, tubelike organ that sticks out from the first part of the large intestine. It has no known function and may be left over from an earlier stage of human evolution.

autoantibody—An antibody that attacks the body's own tissues.

barium—A silvery white metal used to make barium sulfate. When ingested, liquid barium sulfate lets doctors see what the inside of certain organs look like.

bile—A yellowish green fluid made in the liver, stored in the gallbladder, and used in the small intestine to digest fats.

biopsy—A medical procedure in which doctors remove a small amount of tissue from a patient for analysis in a laboratory.

bloating—A symptom of certain digestive disorders in which the person has an uncomfortable feeling of fullness in his or her stomach, which may stick out more than normal.

bowel—Another word for the small and large intestines.

cartilage—Tough, rubbery tissue found in many parts of the body, including the ear, nose, and windpipe, and between bones at joints.

cecum—The first part of the large intestine.

celiac disease—An inherited digestive disorder in which the body is unable to tolerate gluten (a protein).

colic—Sudden, sharp pain in the abdomen.

colon—The part of the large intestine that extends from the cecum to the rectum.

colonoscopy—A medical procedure in which a doctor examines the inside of a person's colon.

constipation—A digestive disorder in which too much water is absorbed from food waste, which becomes hard and compact and difficult to pass through the anus.

Crohn's disease—A type of inflammatory bowel disease that can affect many different parts of the digestive tract.

diarrhea—A digestive disorder in which food passes too quickly through the small intestine before a sufficient amount of water has been absorbed.

duodenum—The first part of the small intestine.

endoscopy—A medical procedure in which the doctor uses a flexible, lighted device to examine the inside of the body, especially the esophagus, stomach, and small intestine.

enema—A medical procedure in which a liquid is inserted into the intestines through the rectum.

enzyme—A type of protein that allows certain chemical reactions to take place within the body.

epiglottis—A flap of cartilage that automatically covers the windpipe when we swallow. The epiglottis keeps food and liquids from going down the windpipe instead of the esophagus.

esophagus—The long passageway that moves food from the mouth and throat and into the stomach.

feces—Solid waste consisting mostly of undigested food.

flare up—A sudden return of painful or uncomfortable symptoms of a digestive disorder such as Crohn's disease.

GERD—The letters that stand for gastroesophageal reflux disease, a digestive disorder in which stomach acids splash back up into the esophagus.

gluten—A protein found in wheat and other grains. Gluten is what makes dough elastic and easy to stretch. It also causes symptoms in people with celiac disease.

Helicobacter pylori—A type of bacteria that can cause ulcers.

hepatitis—Inflammation of the liver.

heredity—A process by which genetic factors are passed on from one generation to the next.

hernia—An abnormal bulging of tissue or an organ through a weakness or tear in a nearby body part.

ileum—The lowest part of the small intestine.

immune system—The body's many ways of recognizing and attacking any harmful organism, cell, or tissue.

inflammatory bowel disease (IBD)—A digestive disorder in which the affected areas of the digestive tract become red and swollen.

irritable bowel syndrome (IBS)—A digestive disorder characterized by repeated bouts of diarrhea and constipation along with cramps and bloating.

lactase—An enzyme produced in the small intestine. Lactase breaks down the lactose found in milk and other diary products.

lactose—A sugar naturally occurring in milk.

lactose intolerance—A digestive disorder in which the body does not produce enough lactase enzyme to break down lactose into simpler, more digestible sugars.

MRI—Magnetic resonance imaging, a powerful tool for taking three-dimensional images of the body's internal organs.

peristalsis—The automatic contraction of muscles that move food and liquids through the entire digestive tract.

rectum—The lowest part of the large intestine and the place where feces are stored prior to a bowel movement.

remission—The disappearance or reduction of the symptoms of a disease.

stool—Another word for feces or solid waste matter from the digestive process.

ulcer—An open sore in the lining of the stomach or some other part of the digestive tract.

ulcerative colitis—A type of inflammatory bowel disease.

villi—Tiny, fingerlike projections that absorb nutrients in the small intestine and pass them into the bloodstream so they can be carried to all parts of the body.

FIND OUT MORE

Books
Betancourt, Marian, and Paul Miskovitz M.D. *The Doctor's Guide to Gastrointestinal Health*. Hoboken, NJ: John Wiley & Sons, Inc., 2005.

Simon, Seymour. *Guts* (Our Digestive System). New York, NY: HarperCollins Publishers, 2005.

Websites
Digestive Disorders (Family Doctor)
http://familydoctor.org/online/famdocen/home/common/digestive.html

Digestive Disorders and Digestive Health Center (WebMD)
www.webmd.com/digestive-disorders/default.htm

Your Digestive System and How It Works
http://digestive.niddk.nih.gov/ddiseases/pubs/yrdd/

Your Stomach & Digestive System
http://kidshealth.org/kid/htbw/digestive_system.html

INDEX

microvilli, 13
milk intolerance, 28, **49**
morphine, 43

opium, 42–43, **43**

pancreas, 14, 16
peppermint, 41–42
peristalsis, 12
plants, 39–40, 41, 42
poppies, **43**
Practical Home Physician (medical text
    book), 37, 38, 42, 43

rectum, 15, 20, **21**, 28, 31, 43

saliva, 11–12
scar tissue, 17, 46
small intestine, **11**, 13–15, 16, 20, 22,
    25, 34–35
    inflammation of, 27–28, **33**, 52
    see also villi
soil, 40
spleen, **11**
stomach, **11**, 12, 13, 16, 21, **34**, 34
stomach acid, **17**, 17, 35, 38
stomach pain, 6, **7**, 8, 30, **37**, 40,
    41–42, 43

treatments
    history of, 36–43
    modern, 7–8, 18, 22, 25, 35, 44–52

ulcerative colitis, 27, 28, 30, 31, 32,
    33
ulcers, 17, **34**, 34–35, 40, 45, 55

villi, 13–14, **14**, 24, 51

worms, 22

George Capaccio enjoys writing books about science and health for young readers. He also likes to make up his own stories and to write poems about things that are important to him. Besides being a writer, George is also a storyteller. He tells folktales and fables from all over the world, mostly in schools and libraries. George lives in Arlington, Massachusetts, with his wife, Nancy, and their beautiful golden retriever. Their dog's name is Habibi, which means "my darling" in Arabic.